Morning Routine:

Skyrocket Your Productivity, Enhance Your Energy & Achieve Your Goals With A Fully Optimized Morning Ritual

Copyright Notice

No part of this book may be reproduced or transmitted in any form whatsoever, electronic, or mechanical, including photocopying, recording, or by any information storage or retrieval system without expressed written, dated and signed permission from the author. All copyrights are reserved.

Disclaimer

Reasonable care has been taken to ensure that the information presented in this book is accurate. However, the reader should understand that the information provided does not constitute legal, medical or professional advice of any kind.

No Liability: this product is supplied "as is" and without warranties. All warranties, express or implied, are hereby disclaimed. Use of this product constitutes acceptance of the "No Liability" policy. If you do not agree with this policy, you are not permitted to use or distribute this product.

We shall not be liable for any losses or damages whatsoever (including, without limitation, consequential loss or damage) directly or indirectly arising from the use of this product.

Rituals Of The Rich & Famous

Success Tips, Strategies and Habits of The Rich & Famous

Get 4 new strategies every week on how to be more productive, confident, and happy.

Get Access Now

Contents

Introduction

Sleep
    Snooze Proof Strategy

Intent

The Boost

Prime Your Mind

Inspiration & Motivation

Mobility

Freshen Up

Breakfast
    Eating Breakfast
    Vitamins
    Whilst You Eat

Most Important Task Of The Day
    Plan Your Day

Conclusion

Introduction

Mornings are the best way to start living the life of your dreams. Starting the day the right way is truly going to determine the remainder of it. Compounded over time that's going to turn into weeks, months and years of successful living. All just from a morning routine!

Many famous successful people credit their successes to a morning routine.

- Barack Obama
  After around five hours of sleep, Barack Obama wakes up. He drinks either orange juice, tea or water and then exercises before eating breakfast. His exercise routine usually involves either strength training or cardio.

- Oprah Winfrey
  The multi billionaire, media company owner Oprah Winfrey likes to rise early at around 5:30 am. She works out for an hour in the gym and then sips on some fruit or vegetable juice before heading off to work.

- Richard Branson
  The founder of the Virgin Group, Richard Branson likes to sleep with the curtains open so that his body clock is

in sync with the earth's natural circadian rhythm. Upon waking he likes to swim in the ocean, kite surf and play tennis. These habits keep him energized to run his huge empire of businesses.

- Arianna Huffington
  Founder and CEO of The Huffington Post, Arianna Huffington likes to get a long sleep. When she wakes up she practices meditation for at least thirty minutes. This keeps her calm and non reactive which is essential for running a demanding business.

You too can be like them! Start carving out some time in the morning and stick to it consistently. It doesn't have to be an hour long. Anything from five minutes is enough. Just decide that whatever it is you choose to do everyday helps you to achieve your goals and have the best state of mind for your life.

To achieve our best results we need to set aside time, each and every morning. We all have our own unique lifestyles. For some of us the morning might start at different times and feature different activities. That's fine, the most important thing is that you choose to implement a consistent routine that will help and guide your actions. In doing so it will also help you to develop the two fundamental essentials of success, focus and discipline.

Get some small wins and stack them up. If you want to meditate thirty minutes a day then dont expect to start with that much. Begin with five minutes or less and work your way up. The same can be applied to any of the other habits you would like to start. Whether that's reading, exercising or anything else important to you, start small. Keep a track of your success on a calendar or in note form. Just mark an "x" on the day and the time. When you stack up the wins it will motivate you to keep going.

Create triggers that remind you to do the things that matter to you in the morning. For example, if reading is important to you, leave a book next to your bedside. Or if exercise is important to you then lay your exercise clothes out the night before. The easier you make it to happen, the more likely you are to engage in the actions.

If you have stronger reasons behind your morning routines then that will help them to stick. Consider each activity on your routine. List the reasons why it is important to you and become aware of them. That could be things such as reading, to become smarter or learning particular things. Or meditating to become calmer and so on. Knowing why your doing these activities will help you to complete them when the going gets tough and also to feel inspired through doing them. On the days that you struggle, remember that when it's hardest is when you form the strongest beliefs and habits.

Now let us take a look at how to optimize your morning routine. Beginning with getting a good nights sleep.

Sleep

Before you even start your morning routine you need to get the best night's sleep possible. Surveys conclude that over fifty percent of Americans are sleep-deprived or regularly have difficulty falling asleep at night. Our sleep debt is impacting our ability to perform at our best. At night, too many of us waste time watching TV, browsing online or just generally wasting time. We need to understand that sleep is a necessity and not a luxury. That doesn't mean that we need to change our entire lives, instead we just need to add in some quality sleep time.

There is a considerable genetic variation in how easy it is for people to get a good night's sleep. The optimal, average range is around seven and a half to nine hours of sleep. The average sleep cycle is ninety minutes long and the average person has five of those. If you put all that together that's about seven and a half hours.

If you can't find enough time at night then naps can help you. In fact we are the only animal that tries to get all of its sleep in one chunk. Every other animal on the planet is multiphasic which means they break up their sleep times. We used to be that way until the industrial revolution. Even back in Roman times people used to block out time for taking a short sleep.

Your body is equipped with a whole bunch of internal clocks that regulate how and when certain processes take place in the body. They operate over a roughly twenty four hour cycle known as the circadian rhythm. There are external cues that influence how these internal clocks work. These cues include things such as bright lights, food intake, movement and stimulants. You can think of your circadian rhythm as the source code for a software which contains the individual commands that are regulating how the software is working. Any time you input a command into the source code, such as drinking a cup of coffee or exposure to bright light, you're inputting another entry into the source code.Now what your body wants is to have these commands to be as consistent and predictable as possible. That's why it is important to have a consistent sleep schedule.

The first step is to figure out your bedtime. Understand that the amount of sleep we need is roughly around seven and a half hours. In order to get to that we have to be able to schedule our bedtime based on our wake-up time. Wakeup times are determined by work and commitments. Decide on what that is and then stick to it. Once you have your wake up time count backwards from that seven and a half hours.

Everything you do over the course of the day is going to contribute to your quality of sleep in some way either positively or negatively. The first step is to create a really big contrast between the first half of your day and the second part of your day. The bigger this contrast is the more you are going to condition yourself to be relaxed and still when the time for sleep comes.

Daytime is the time to be exposed to a lot of stimulation such as bright lights, social interactions, movement and physical activity. It is the time to get your stressful errands handled, to work hard and get things done. Nighttime on the other hand is the time to let go, to be relaxed, peaceful and just generally wind down.

At night, minimize your exposure to light and in particular blue light because it sends a strong signal to your body that it should be alert and awake. It also suppresses melatonin production which is the hormone that your body produces as you're getting ready to sleep.

Tweak the light bulbs you have at home. You can buy incandescent light bulbs which emit a lower spectrum of light and less of the blue light. Tweak your smartphone and laptop screens to emit less blue light. There are applications which will optimize your devices for this. Alternatively you can buy some blue light blocking glasses which have more orange or red tinted lenses and they will do the job of blocking blue light as well.

During the daytime having lots of blue light is actually a good thing because it's helping to reinforce this big contrast between your daytime and your nighttime. A few things you can do specifically is to get outside as much as possible during the daylight hours. Now for many of us that is only possible to an extent because we are having to spend a lot of time indoors. Particularly if you have an office job. But even going to the nearest balcony every hour or so and spending a few minutes outside is already going to help you.

Besides light, the next thing to be aware of is caffeine. Consider the amount of time for the peak concentration of caffeine in your blood. In the case of caffeine it's about five or six hours which means that you want to space out your caffeine intake sufficiently far enough from your bedtime. Ideally have your last caffeine dose ten hours before bedtime. Substances like chocolate, tea and cocoa powder also contain caffeine so be aware of those too.

Anxiety and stress are another big reason people give for why their sleep is disrupted. Find out how to flip the off switch in your mind so that you're not thinking about things when you should be sleeping. Now flipping that switch is not easy. To help you need to create a buffer zone where you slowly calm down via rituals.

Stress is unavoidable, it is a part of life and some amount of it is actually even beneficial because it helps you to be more alert and productive. High amounts of stress at certain parts of the day is fine. But at night you need very low amounts of it. Therefore you should do the hardest thing first thing in the morning and then progress to easier activities as the day goes on. So for example if you have some stressful issues, deal with all of those early in the day and don't leave it too late. The same applies for socializing. Have easy interactions late on and save the debates for early on.

Avoid distractions like social media a few hours before bed because they can trigger you to be more alert and awake. For example responding to messages or comments. Practice solitude and spending time alone with your thoughts.

Nowadays we are constantly connected. What your brain does when it's just and your thoughts is to try to creatively solve problems and conclusions. The worst time to do all of that is the time when you actually want to fall asleep. So it is important to have dedicated times during the day when you are not listening to a podcast or looking at your phone. It should be just you and your thoughts.

Implement relaxing time into your day by for example, having a couple of commutes where your not doing anything. Or taking a break to sit on a park bench. Or taking an evening walk to reflect and let your brain solve problems. Similar practices that are also effective are journaling or exercising. That could just be stream of consciousness journaling where you literally write your thoughts. Your brain needs to process all the information it receives. Jamming it with social media is filling it up with even more thought loops.

The best way to alleviate stress from any kind of pressing issue is to try to fix the problem and actively do something about it. Don't just hope that the problem goes away. There is a good chance that it won't happen. When you actively try to deal with the stress there is a higher chance that you won't be bothered by it for as long. Exercise and movement in general are excellent for helping with sleep issues. If you can exercise early in the day that might be even better. The only thing to be mindful of here is that you don't want to have a lot of stimulants before.

We also need to make our room a sanctuary cool, dark and mellow. There's an optimal temperature range for sleep.

Cooler temperatures are better for sleeping. Higher body temperatures are associated with wakefulness in your body. Your body temperature is naturally going through fluctuations over the course of the day where it hits a peak at some point during the daylight hours and then it gradually goes down as your sleep time approaches. If your room is very warm that might mess with your sleep. In the winter, that's not a big issue because you can just turn down the heating. In the summer this can be trickier so an AC can help but of course that can be tough on your electricity bill. A cheaper option is to have a ventilator or a fan which is directed towards you.

Then you want your bedroom to be as dark as possible. Our pineal gland and skin are sensitive to light when sleeping so it's very important that it's dark in your room. Ideally you should not even be able to see your hands in front of you. Now this is not that easy to do all the time because maybe you're renting an Airbnb where they don't have blackout curtains. But you can buy some global sticky curtain things or even black bin bag tape up the windows. Add to that an eye mask and your good to go.

Finally, be aware of noise. It;s a good idea to sleep with earplugs in just in case there are any noises during the night. It's super annoying when you finally fall asleep and then some sudden noise wakes you up. If you don't have earplugs then putting in some sort of white noise into your ear helps. You can find a lot of these on YouTube or just download them. Even listening to some sort of speech, podcast or interview can also help during sleeping. If someone is speaking with a very soothing kind of calm tone it just helps you to drift away and fall asleep.

The reality is is that part of living on planet Earth is that sometimes there is value in things that are not completely coinciding with your health optimization quest. For example you might want to go out on a late night date. Or party with friends on the weekend. There can be value to these things and sometimes a thing that might be great for your overall life experience might not be the best thing for your sleep. In general try to get good sleep but every once in a while it might be worth it to do something that goes against that but has more value to you in another area of life.

Snooze Proof Strategy

The alarm goes off and you hit the snooze button for some more minutes in bed. But are those extra minutes in bed actually going to help you? In fact our bodies have chemical mechanisms that will wake us up naturally, without an alarm clock.

Approximately one hour before you wake up the body begins to prepare. Hormones such as cortisol and dopamine are released to give you energy. The problem with an alarm is that it interrupts the natural cycle.

When the alarm goes off your body might not be quite ready to wake up. Oftentimes you will feel groggy and tired, which is a state known as "sleep inertia". The deeper your sleep the stronger the sleep inertia. During this state is when we are more likely to hit the snooze button. But this can do more damage to you than good because when you hit the snooze button your body starts to go back into deeper sleep cycles. Instead of preparing to wake up it is going back to sleep and making things worse.

Here you enter into a vicious cycle. Ultimately it's better not to snooze and if you need to, just set the alarm a bit later. Plus you move your alarm or phone to the other side of the room. Then you will have to get out of bed to turn it off! Try to resist the temptation to snooze and stack up the wins. If you can win the first part of the day your well on your way to success. As the saying goes, if you snooze you lose.

Another thing upon waking that you need to be aware of is checking your phone first thing. Doing this will just put you into a reactive mode all day where your not actually in control of your life. Instead spend some time in the mornings to do your routine.

No checking your emails or social media in the morning. It can distract you and set your mood for the rest of the day. You might come across something negative and then it's going to mess up your day.

Sure there'll be some mornings where you actually have to check something and that's okays. Overall you need to learn to live in the present and enjoy your morning doing what you enjoy the most and doing what sets you up for the day. To help you implement this habit put your phone on airplane mode when sleeping so that when you wake up you won't be distracted by all the notifications.

Intent

Begin each day with a positive intent. That might sound hard to do when Monday morning rolls in too quickly. Your already stressed just thinking about heading to the office and taking care of all the things you need to do. However there is good news because you can make some small changes that will help you to deal with life more effectively and in turn make you a happier person.

Smile

As soon as you wake up, start the day with a smile. Force yourself to smile even if you don't want to because not only does it set a positive intention, it also lowers blood pressure and strengthens your immune system. Start the day right and start it with a smile.

Goals

Keep rolling with a positive intent. Sit up and write out your top goals on a piece of paper. This will bring them into your awareness and again set a positive intent for the day ahead. Always keep a pen and notepad at the side of your bed. Writing by hand will send the goals deeper into your subconscious mind. This is one of the most effective tools to focus your thoughts every day and to set the intention for where you're going to go. It really works, if you think about the color red then all you see is red when you look around the room. Think about your goals and the more opportunities you will see. Planting your goals into your mind when its freshest is the best way to establish them.

Take your goals for the week and phrase them as if they already happened. For example, instead of saying "I set a goal to make $10,000 this week" write out "I made $10,000 this week". Write it out ten or fifteen times in a row on a piece of paper. Do that for two or three areas of your life. You can write down exactly what has happened this week, before if actually even happened. Write down specifically what you want in life as if it has already happened.

I am one of the top sellers in my company
I look and feel ten years younger
I worked out five times this week.
I only fly first class

If you haven't set any goals for your life then this time can be used to figure them out. Write anything you want for thirty days and then analyze the results at the end of the month. Write goals for your health, wealth, career, mind, friends, relationships, travel and adventure. Notice any recurring themes and then those are your goals. Focus on them, break them down and send them into your subconscious mind everyday.

Once you have written your goals it's time to get out of bed!

The Boost

Water

Almost all of your body is composed of water. When you are not taking in water everything in your body is getting dehydrated. After a long nights sleep you will be dehydrated and so in the morning you need to rehydrate right away. Drinking water first thing will hydrate you and speed up your metabolism, especially with cold water. Cold water will boost your body with energy, get the engines rolling and also help to flush out any toxins. Put the coffee down, you can have it later on.

Adding lemon to your water is a great way to boost your immunity. It also contains various healthy minerals and serves as more than enough for your daily recommendation of Vitamin C. This is essential for taking care of vital organs such as the liver. Mix it up with some pink himalayan salt to further boost immunity, improve digestion and balance your body.

This simple cocktail can improve health, vitality and wellness. It will pull the toxins from your cells, giving you better skin and optimal body functioning.

Brush Your Teeth

We all know the benefits of brushing your teeth. Making this a habit of being one of the first things you do is a great way to build your self esteem and respect. Besides that, morning breath can be pretty terrible!

Another benefit to brushing your teeth right away is that it removes any bacteria from your mouth that has accumulated over night. During sleep saliva production which allows bacteria to multiply can eat away at your teeth. Brushing your teeth first thing quickly gets rid of it. Incidentally, this really is the most important time to brush your teeth. Spend time brushing each and every tooth in your mouth. Don't rush through the process, you should take at least two minutes in order to thoroughly clean your teeth. Use mouthwash to rinse off.

Prime Your Mind

The mind is at its freshest in the morning. What you do during this time will have a huge impact on your day. Repeated regularly, it starts to dictate the outcome of your life. Take responsibility and prime your mind for success. A peaceful non reactive mind is one of the best mindstates for us to have. Welcome joy and happiness into your life.

Meditation

Start the day peacefully with meditation and it will carry through your day. In recent times, meditation has become a popular habit. These days there are many applications, courses and classes that teach meditation. It is a powerful practice that can help reduce depression, anxiety and various mental health issues. You don't need to be a monk or a spiritual person to gain the benefits of meditation. It works the same for all of us and it doesn't matter who you are or what you do.

Regular meditation enhances your brain and helps you to deal with stress much more effectively. Not only that but it provides numerous mental health benefits from concentration to calmness and much more. Scientists have also observed that meditation causes your brain to release endorphins. These are the chemicals that make us feel good.

Morning is the best time for meditation because your mind is alert and less prone to distractions. There is less stress at this time of day, especially if you have followed the morning routine and not used your phone yet. If you need more time for meditation, then wake up a little bit earlier. If your too busy then that means you really need it! You will be grateful for all the benefits it provides.

To begin, sit in a comfortable place that is quiet and free from distractions. The best position is to sit cross legged. But if that's uncomfortable for you then you can lie down or sit in a chair. Wear some comfortable clothes and have the right temperature setting. You don't want to be getting up or moving around during your meditation sessions. Some people find value from further blocking out noise and light using eye masks and noise cancelling headphones. These will really allow you to go into a deep meditative state. Try them if you like.

Set a timer on your phone and turn the data off. If your a beginner, start with five minutes and then after some weeks or months of practice, increase the time. The best results come from fifteen to thirty minute sessions. Eyes can be open or closed as you wish. Then you simply breathe in and out. Focus on your breath going in and out of your body. Relax and let your breath flow. Allow your breathing to find its rhythm. Just be.

Stay like this until your alarm goes off. If thoughts enter into your mind, just watch them pass by. If you catch yourself engaging in thoughts then become aware, let them go and come back again to your breathing. If a sound or anything else distracts you let it go and again come back to your breathing.

There are many more styles of mediation. Some involve focusing on breathing whilst others repeat words/mantras and then some even combine meditation with yoga. It's a huge subject and has only been covered briefly here. If your interested to learn more then I suggest checking out some YouTube videos or study a course.

Breathing Exercises

Breathing exercises in the morning can be a great way to wake you up and infuse your body with energy. The most notable breathing exercise right now is The Wim Hof Method. As a result of consistently exposing himself to extreme cold and heat Wim Hof developed the method to withstand such conditions.

To begin get comfortable, you can sit in a crossed legged position or whatever your feel the most comfortable with. Just make sure that your lungs can expand without and restriction. For best results practice when your stomach is empty.

1. Power

Close your eyes. Follow the same style of powerful short bursts of breathing as if you were blowing up a balloon. Inhale through the nose and exhale through the mouth. Maintain a consistent rhythm and allow your stomach to follow. Repeat for around thirty breaths. During this you might feel light headed, don't worry it's normal.

2. Hold

After completing thirty rapid breaths, take in a deep breath to fill the lungs. Let the air out and then at the end hold it for as long as possible. Eventually you will feel the gasp reflex. If you want to, you can add some push ups whilst holding your breath. This will build your strength.

3. Recover

Bring the breath back in to fill your lungs and feel your chest expand. When you are filled with air hold the breath for about ten seconds. This completes one round. Repeat for three rounds in succession.

The three steps process can be repeated in a cycle for around three rounds. After completion take some time to relax and enjoy the feeling.

In addition to The Wim Hoff method or instead of it you can try Tony Robbins breathing technique. This enfuses your body with energy. If you wake up feeling groggy and sluggish try it out. Simple raise and lower your hands above your head as you breath in and out explosively. In through the nose out through the mouth. Repeat for thirty times and do three rounds. In between each round jump lightly up and down and hum for ten to twenty times. Your body will wake up for sure.

Prayer

A short prayer is a beautiful way to focus your time and attention. You don't need to be religious, this could be a prayer to yourself, family, friends or seeking God's advice for the day ahead. Prayer centers us, begins the day with positivity and a focus on your higher self.

Follow the prayers in The Bible or print some out. Personally I have adapted my own over the years. You can do the same. Mine simply gives thanks to my creators, my family god and to wish for health, happiness and success in my goals. Finally I ask for blessings for the people I love and once again give thanks.

"Dear Lord, Farther, Jesus, God.

Thank you for blessing me with this life, family, friends, health, success, love and happiness.
Please guide me to becoming the strongest version of myself today and for the rest of my days. Bless me with love, success, happiness and prosperity in your kingdom.
Please watch over the people I love and help us to live our best lives."

Visualisation

After your prayers a short visualization session will help you to manifest your goals and dreams. That could be for the forthcoming day, week, year or even from your grand vision.

Now there's some big big myths around visualization. First, most people think that when you visualize something it should look exactly like it does in real life. This is where people get demotivated and give up. In fact, it's never like that for anybody.

Instead let me share with you a very simple and highly effective process. First of all, get clear about what your intention is. You need to plant that intention like a seed in the soil of the universe. It will grow as nature will take its course.

Start with the emotion. How will it feel to have the situation, circumstance, person, opportunity or whatever it is you want? How would you behave, how would you sit, stand, walk? Close your eyes and get in touch with the feeling. Out of the feeling images will arise. They might be vague and probably aren't going to look like real life but that's fine, as long as you're connected to the feelings.

The whole process for each goal only needs to be fifteen to thirty seconds at a time. It is not something you need to be pounding the universe with. Because it certainly knows how to respond to your thought energy and emotions. Thoughts create actions. Actions create energy and energy turns into reality.

Affirmations

What if you could somehow brainwash yourself to become successful? Affirmations can help you. They only take a few minutes and can be combined with some physical activity such as walking or yoga. An affirmation is a positive statement that you repeat to yourself which describes how you want to be.

There is a common misconception that affirmations are just like magic pills that make things happen with no effort. This is commonly found in the people who are looking for the easy way or have heard about the power of affirmations. First of all understand that it is action which brings about changes in people's lives. Affirmations are there to help motivate you into taking more action. The more action you begin to take the more the universe is going to work in your favor. Energy responds to like energy and our entire universe is comprised of energy. The more action you take, the more energy you produce. That comes in the form of people, places, circumstances or events that are all designed to help get you closer to your goal.

In order for affirmations to work you need consistency. Affirmations are so easy to forget to do that people end up only doing them sometimes. Also affirmations produce little to no immediate results so people end up giving up because they're not getting the results they want fast enough. Anything worth achieving requires consistency. Affirmations can lead you to your goals so stick with them.

Now the affirmation might not be true but over time it starts to sink into your subconscious which starts to believe it. Essentially you create a self-fulfilling prophecy. Sounds pretty easy right, so then why doesn't it work for some people?

Reason number one is that their affirmations are too unbelievably positive. If I keep telling myself "I am a millionaire, I am a millionaire, I am a millionaire". But your living in grandma's basement eating noodles every night there's a good chance that your conscious brain is going to reject that affirmation. When the conscious rejects it the subconscious rejects it and then it doesn't materialize into your life.

In order for affirmations to work, they first need to be believable to the conscious brain. That way there's little to no resistance. Now it's not that you'll never be able to affirm things like "I'm a millionaire" or something even bigger. What it means is that you need to focus first on making your affirmations small and believable. The more small and believable the affirmations are, the more progress you're going to make. The more progress you make, the more confident you're going to feel in your ability to start asking for bigger and better things.

When it comes time to affirmations your conscious brain is your best friend and it's also your worst enemy. So if you say to yourself something like, "I'm going to be a millionaire" it's going to be like when I'm ninety years old or I'll probably be dead by the time. For that exact reason you want your affirmations to be specific and believable.

Start making affirmations work for you. Forming them in the present tense makes them more believable. Take your goals or mind states that will help you to achieve them. For example:

I am earning 10,000 usd per month online by november this year
I am in a happy relationship by october this year
I am confident and outgoing
I look and feel amazing

Write down your affirmations in a little notebook and carry them with you everywhere that you go. That way you can pull them out and refer to them throughout the day and every morning. It's very very helpful to keep reminding yourself of what it is you're after. This will help you to take more action towards making those dreams come true.

Another thing you can do is to write all of your affirmations on post-it notes and place them all throughout the house or the common areas that you frequent the most. When you wake up, have your subconscious brain absorb those affirmations.

They will really change your life.

Inspiration & Motivation

Instead of starting your day consuming social media or news try feeding your mind with positive information.

Reading

Spend at least ten minutes in the morning reading a book. There's something about reading that really helps your mind with making better decisions. The beautiful thing about doing it each and every day is that you set yourself up to make better decisions throughout the day.

Its well known that some of the most successful entrepreneurs and business leaders are avid readers. Including Mark Zuckerberg, Bill Gates, Mahatma Gandhi, Emma Watson and many more.

Reading has been proven to significantly reduce stress levels, enhance brain power and lower anxiety and depression. Plus all the learning and escapology for your mind. All you need to do is read for a minimum of six minutes per day to start to gain the benefits. In fact, it's often a better alternative to listening to music or going for a walk. Plus if you read for upto thirty minutes a day you can even start to add years to your life!

The most successful and wealthy people prefer educational material and tend to read non fiction books. Biographies of successful people are particularly popular with them. However many also enjoy fiction, particularly at night because it helps them to unwind and sleep. In addition reading fiction has the power to increase emotional intelligence. In conclusion reading can significantly change your life for the better, so make it a habit and part of your mornings.

Quotes

If reading a book is a bit too much try reading some simple quotes. You can find literally millions of quotes online. Quotes will lift your spirits and motivate you for the day ahead. Go ahead and find some online, print them off or write them down somewhere you can look at every morning.

Gratitude

Gratitude is a simple way to bring to your attention the things in your life that mean something to you. With such a strong emotion in your heart, it's harder to fall into negative thinking. Bring gratitude into your awareness every morning with gratitude journaling.

The premise gratitude journaling is to list out several different things that you are grateful for. Be as detailed as possible with whatever it is that you're grateful for. By doing this you are shifting your thoughts into positive directions. When you are aware of all that you have instead of being focused on the have-nots. Focus on the good, especially when you are going through difficult times. Later you can flip back to any given day and read what it is you are grateful for.

Gratitude journaling takes just a few minutes to do in the morning. Try the five minute journal out. Simply record three to five things your grateful for each day. Reflect on your life and count your blessings.

Journal

Another tool you can use to change your life is journaling. This is a cool way that you can coach yourself. You can go back to get insights so you don't lose them and continue to evolve.

There are a number of ways you can journal. Once of the most beneficial and easiest to follow is stream of consciousness journaling. As the name relays it means literally writing down your thoughts without censoring them. Put pen to paper and don't stop writing. You can either set a timer for five minutes or more. Alternatively you can set a page count, say three pages and then stop. That's all there is to it. No editing or going back. Just put down on paper whatever is on your mind.

The purpose of journaling is to free up your mind so there is nothing weighing it down for the day ahead. This method has been proven to help with depression and to organize thoughts. Oftentimes we get stuck in a circle of negative thoughts or something is bothering us at the back of our minds. Putting it down on paper releases you from it. In addition when we sleep our brain resolves things we went to sleep thinking about. Journaling in the morning will help to bring more clarity to any ongoing issues you have.

Have no filter when you write. You don't need to look back on it. Essentially its therapy for your mind. You can even be negative and complain here if you like. Get it all off your chest. It's better than putting that out into the world in the form of gossip or complaining. Just make sure no one ever reads it! Put your most honest thoughts on there. Even your darkest secrets, fears, fantasies or negative thoughts. You might find that you don't necessarily agree with them. Eckart tolle is often quoted as saying we are not our thoughts. This process will help you to see what is real and what is bs in your mind. Unblock your mind with journaling.

If you want to start journaling in the morning then set aside the time to do it. Journaling should take from ten to forty minutes. The more the better. But of course we all have a finite amount of time. The time you spend on journaling will pay off though so maybe get up a bit earlier to do it.

Make sure you use a pen and paper since it is much more effective and you should avoid any screens during the first hours of your day. There are many applications and word processors that can help you to digitally capture your notes. Speed isn't something you should be concerned with here. Even if your writing sucks just take more time on it. When you write longhand it catches more of your thoughts. It also keeps a fresh mental break from the digital world.

Mobility

After sleeping for a good seven to nine hours your body will be quite stiff and in need of some stretching. Yoga and Tai Chi are both great ways to start moving your body. Once you start practicing them regularly in the morning, your body will become accustomed to waking up much more easily. Which means you will feel more awake and energized.

Yoga

Yoga is a very easy exercise to learn. Long term practice helps to maintain a healthy body and mind. You don't need to take a full class to get the benefits. Ten minutes or more is plenty. Even on the days where you feel tired and groggy simply doing some basic yoga will put you into the right state of mind.

The practice of morning yoga will warm up your body helping the blood and nutrients to flow through it. This helps to alleviate aches, pains and promote a better posture. All of which strengthen your immune system for better health and mobility. Combined with a focus on breathing it stimulates your body and wakes up your brain. It's almost like having a fresh cup of coffee but without the side effects!

If you work at a desk or sit for long hours during the day then your body craves the stretching that yoga offers. It will set your body up for a better strength during the day.

You can learn some basic Yoga on YouTube. Load a video and follow along. Learn some basic poses and then everyday, practice the ones that suit you the best.

Tai Chi

If yoga doesn't fit with you then Tai Chi can be a great alternative. Or you could even practice some martial arts drills from Muay Thai, Jiu Jitsu and so on.

Tai Chi is a traditional Chinese exercise that is based in martial arts and involves slow movements combined with deep breathing. Learning it is quite easy. As we have discussed movement and breathing promote various health benefits. Both physical and emotional. Reducing stress and anxiety is one of the biggest benefits of Tai Chi. Numerous studies have concluded this fact. Since Tai Chi also incorporates a form of meditation with exercise it has a great advantage. All this will help to improve your mood, health and sleep whilst alleviating negativity and ill health.

Tai Chi is accessible to all ages. When your starting out you may experience some aches and pains but after more practice those will go away to make you become stronger. As you progress, pay attention to proper posture and precision. It might help to study on Youtube, get an instructor or take a few classes to learn the basics. There are a few different styles of Tai Chi so experiment with them and try the one that feels right for you.

Both Tai Chi and yoga involve meditation and movement. Therefore they have similar benefits and are an excellent addition to your morning routine. All you need is ten minutes a day. Start practicing one of them every morning and celebrate your improved health and happiness.

Exercise

Besides yoga and Tai Chi there are a number of other ways you can work out in the morning. The two most popular are of course weightlifting and running. Health experts recommend mixing aerobic (running/cardio) with anaerobic (weightlifting/strength training). Aerobic exercise uses oxygen on a steady supply whilst anaerobic uses more short bursts. You can choose either or both for your morning.

Weight Lifting/Strength Training

The best time to hit the gym is first thing in the day. This gets it done and out of the way. It also sets a positive tone for the day by breaking through early resistance.

When you wake up hormone levels, particularly testosterone are at their peak. These help you build muscle mass much quicker. Taking advantage of high levels is a great way to get ripped and muscular. Working out early on will also boost your metabolism which plays a vital role in burning fat. This allows your body to burn more calories, even when your not exercising.

Get your workout in early in the day. You will be more free from distractions and the crowds will be smaller. After work it will be much harder to summon the willpower to go. So do it while you can and whilst your body is best wired for it. Then you can go on and enjoy your day including quality time with your loved ones.

But it's not always going to be easy to motivate yourself. So here are some tips to help you go to the gym, first thing. Prepare your clothes and everything you will need the night before. Pack all your gym clothes, protein, towel and anything else you might need. This will lower the resistance to going. Plus the decision has already been made in your mind.

Make sure you keep working on your motivation to hit the gym. That might be a goal to reach a certain weight, look a certain way or feel better. It could even be avoiding going to the gym when it's busy. Sometimes all you need to do is just show up.

Morning Run

Getting out of bed in the morning is hard enough, let alone trying to go for a run! However there are a number of great benefits to a morning run and you don't need to be an Olympic athlete to reap the rewards of morning running. More energy, focus, better sleep and weight loss being some of the biggest benefits. Plus you will feel great that you have already worked out before the demands of the day starts.

When you begin a regular routine of running in the morning your body clock will start to adjust and you will wake up easier. At the start it's going to be hard and you will feel sluggish. But go ahead and persevere!

There are some great tricks you can use to help you start running in the morning. Spike your sugar and energy levels with a banana before running. Or drink a cup of tea or coffee to give you that boost for the run. Have your running shoes and clothes laid out the night before so there are fewer barriers between you and getting on with the run. Do a short stretching session to warm up your muscles and put you in the right mood. When you begin the run you can start slowly. Eventually you will begin to wake up and pick up the pace. Keep a record of your runs and have some goals to reach. Listen to some music whilst you run and get inspired.

Freshen Up

After some good stretching and exercise you will have worked up a little sweat. Also during night your likely to sweat. A good shower is not only cleaning and cleansing, it also improve various bodily functions.

These days there is a lot of debate as to the benefits of hot showers versus cold showers.

Hot Showers

Hot showers can help to rejuvenate muscles. If your regularly lifting heavy weights then a hot shower could be a good idea for you. They also improve blood circulation which will help to ease pain and reduce inflammation. In addition if your suffering from a case of the flu or a blocked nose then a hot shower can help to unblock your sinuses. Furthermore pores in the skin are softened and unclogged with the steam from a hot shower. This leaves a much cleaner and smoother skin surface.

Cold Showers

Cold showers are a bit daunting first thing in the morning but there are a number of benefits to them. Psychologically they are going to build willpower. Overcoming the fear to jump into that cold shower will help you considerably when you face challenges in your life. Then there are the health benefits. Cold water helps to close the pores of your skin which makes it much more firm and appear youthful. It also makes hair stronger. Immunity and blood circulation are also improved as a result of cold showering. This can help to speed up recovery.

Now after all that you might be confused as to what temperature to set your shower! The best way is to choose a temperature that feels the most beneficial to you. However there are times when one can be more beneficial than the other. If you suffer from insomnia a hot shower will adjust your body for a better sleep. If you are prone to acne then cold showers will be better since they close skin pores. If you suffer from cramps then a warm shower will help your muscles to relax. In addition, you can also alternate between cold and hot showers to improve blood circulation and detox your body.

Questions

Your level of happiness and fulfilment is not based on your circumstances but instead on how you perceive your circumstances through your own mental and emotional filters.

These filters are shaped by various factors including, culture, upbringing, religion, experiences and values. Who you believe you are and your story of yourself are influenced by these factors.

We can begin to change our habits and perceptions for the better by rewriting these filters. The most effective way to do that is by asking ourselves better questions. When you begin to consistently ask better questions your perception of your circumstances will change.

Instead of focusing on what you lack or what you want from someone focus on what you can give or what makes you happy. Encourage yourself to find ways to overcome obstacles and plateaus in your life. Identify where you can improve and how. Questions can help you with all of this and much more. Raise the quality of your life with quality questions.

When taking a shower its a great time to ask some questions that will enhance your state and focus your attention on the things that matter the most to you. Questions stimulate thought and motivate you. Here are some questions you can ask and answer out loud to yourself.

- *What am I grateful for? How does that make me feel?*
- *What am I proud of? How does that make me feel?*

- *How can I add more value to the world today?*
- *Who do I love? Who loves me?*
- *What is a decision I can make that would remove a hundred other decisions?*
- *What if I did the opposite for today?*
- *What is the worst that could happen? Could I get back from there?*
- *If I could only work 2 hours per week on my business what would I do?*
- *What would this look like if it were easy?*

Breakfast

Many people believe that breakfast is the most important meal of the day. But did you know that you can lose fat and increase muscle mass with fasting?

The most popular fasting method right now is intermittent fasting which typically involves eating all of your meals during an eight hour window. For the other sixteen hours you don't eat anything. It's actually pretty easy to incorporate into your life since for eight hours your asleep anyway. That usually means skipping breakfast and late night meals. For example if your last meal is at 8pm, you sleep at midnight and wake up at 8 am. In that case your first meal would be at 12pm. Each of our schedules are going to be different so you can adjust those times to suit yours.

Intermittent fasting is not a diet, it's a way of scheduling your eating so that you get the most benefits. Which is a great way for you to become more lean without having to worry about what you eat. Whenever your body is full and in a fed state it is very hard to burn fat. Normally your body takes three to five hours to absorb and digest food. After that time you enter into a fasted state where insulin levels are much lower which makes it easier for your body to burn fat.

Diets long term are more difficult to stick to because they soon become tedious based on the limitation of only certain foods. Intermittent fasting, on the other hand can quickly become an easy lifestyle change to implement since it only requires thinking about consuming food within a set time period.

Losing fat is just one of the main benefits of intermittent fasting. It also makes your day much more simple to plan. Not only that but you save time in the morning since you don't have to worry about breakfast. Studies have even found that intermittent fasting can lead to longer lifespans. In particular, a lot of research has studied the relationship between cancer and fasting. Patients showed signs of reduction in cancer when fasting.

There are a few different ways to go with intermittent fasting. You can try one day of normal eating, no time restrictions and then the next day a full twenty four hour fast. Or you can go with the first method explained, eat for eight hours and fast for sixteen hours.

The mental barrier is the main obstacle to people trying fasting because in reality it's not that hard. You might be concerned about skipping breakfast and maybe you love breakfast foods. So just delay them.

You can learn more about intermittent fasting by reading and watching materials, but the best way to learn is to experiment.

Eating Breakfast

If your still concerned about your weight but don't want to try intermittent fasting then eat a healthy breakfast instead. Eating breakfast can be good too because it breaks the nighttime fast and kick-starts your metabolism.

A healthy breakfast should contain nutrition, fill you up and provide enough energy for the day ahead. Here are some of the best foods to get you going.

Oatmeal

Oatmeal is loaded with nutrition and keeps you feeling full for hours. Oats contain powerful antioxidants, protein and fiber. These are great for building a strong body and providing lots of energy. Add in some fruits and almond milk. A great way to begin the day.

Eggs

Eggs are a popular breakfast choice. They are clean, nutritious and full of protein. If you're counting your carbs then eggs are a great choice. Serve them scrambled, poached, fried or boiled.

Nuts & nut butter

If you are vegan or vegetarian then eating nuts is a great alternative source of protein and natural healthy fats. Nuts are also rich in antioxidants which can help you live longer if consumed regularly. Serve some nut butter on your toast or mix them in with some fruits.

Coffee

A cup of coffee in the morning is another popular breakfast choice because it gives you a kick start. If your doing intermittent fasting coffee can also help to stave off hunger in the mornings. Choose decaffeinated coffee and you decrease any health risks. Also avoid adding any cream or sugar. Americanos and espressos all the way.

Tea

If your not into coffee but still need a little bit more energy in the mornings than tea can help you. Tea also contains many powerful antioxidants which support your immune system and promote long term health.

Fruits

All kinds of fruits are an excellent start to the morning. Most are low in calories and jam packed full of valuable nutrients and vitamins which help fight diseases. Add them to your cereal, oatmeal, yoghurt or eat them on their own. You could even blend them as a smoothie.

Flaxseed

Flaxseeds can be sprinkled onto your yoghurt, oatmeal or cereal. They protein, fiber and omega 3. This can help to lower cholesterol and improve blood sugar levels. Make sure to grind the seeds down so they can pass through the body without breaking down.

Cereal

There are millions of cereals out there. Just choose one that has some great nutritional content and you're good to go. Avoid anything that is too processed or loaded with chemicals and sugars. Sugars will spike your energy but leave you crashing later on.

Greek yogurt

Greek yogurt is a great source of protein. It also contains calcium and probiotics which support a healthy gut and immune system.

Cottage cheese

If you're looking for another source of protein than cottage cheese is loaded with it. It can also stave off hunger for longer. You can eat it by itself or it goes well with peppers, dried fruits and nuts.

Vitamins

Get some vitamins into your body first thing to set your engines rolling. There are millions of vitamins out there. Choose the ones that you think will add value to your life. Also make sure to choose high quality ones from trusted companies. Check the reviews. Here are some of the best.

Protein

Besides being great for building muscle a protein shake in the morning is a convenient and healthy option. Even better if your travelling since you won't have to worry about having to find decent food or spending too much money on breakfast.

Mix up some protein with milk, water or even almond milk. Give your digestion a rest and supplement it for food as being a liquid breakfast. Choose protein powders that are low in sugar and preferably dairy free.

Gingko

Ginkgo (Ginkgo biloba) is an extract taken from the leaves of one of the oldest living tree species. They help to improve blood circulation due to their powerful antioxidant qualities. Also it has often been associated with improving memory. They can be taken in tablet, capsule forms or even drank in tea.

Spirulina

Spirulina is a microalgae with lots of nutritional value and health benefits. According to the National Institutes of Health (NIH) Spirulina is promoted as helping with various health issues including weight loss, heart health, diabetes, mental and general wellbeing. Combined with zinc it can help cleanse the body. Can be taken in powder diluted with water or capsule.

Apple cider vinegar

Apple cider vinegar has been around for centuries. Weight loss, improved circulation, immune healing and digestion are just a few of its claimed health benefits. Mix one to two tablespoons with water every morning before you eat anything.

Turmeric

Turmeric is another supplement that can be taken to help with improving digestion and inflammation. Inflammation is one of the biggest issues people have when it comes to their health. Mix about a teaspoon of turmeric with water and it is more than enough.

Gelatin/Collagen hydrolysate

This is good for your joints specifically connective tissue repair to make sure you don't have any injuries and recover quicker. Protect your joints before it's too late. One to two tablespoons of this will serve you well.

Fiber

Fiber is a really important part of your diet. Fiber helps to improve digestion which is a massive part of how your body functions. There are various capsules or even chewy tablets available. Go with the ones which digest the easiest.

Multivitamins

There's a lot of debate out there about whether or not multivitamins vitamins are worth taking because a lot of people think that you don't absorb them. The best way to tell is to experiment with different ones. Check reviews and also observe if your urine is looking any different when you take them. If it does look different than usually that's because your urinating the vitamins out and the body is not absorbing them. Find ones that don't just flush out of your body.

A good multivitamin should contain all the important vitamins. Including Vitamin A for immune function. Vitamin B for health and energy. Vitamin C for preventing and treating colds and Vitamin D for strong bones.

Omega-3 fish oils

Omega-3 fish oil are loaded with docosahexaenoic acid (DHA) and eicosapentaenoic acid (EPA). These are important and beneficial for overall heart health. They also help to lower blood pressure and reduce heart diseases or attacks which are extremely common these days. Everyone should eat fish at least twice a week because they are high in omega-3 fatty acids. For those who do not like eating fish Omega-3 fish oils are a great alternative.

Tribulus

Another natural supplement. This one is for the men because it helps with boosting testosterone, libido and stamina. Research has concluded that men's sexual desire increased by over seventy percent after consuming Tribulus for two months. Take one to two capsules a day.

Creatine

Creatine is a supplement which helps to improve strength and performance in the gym. Various studies have concluded that it can increase muscle size, strength and exercise performance. In addition it helps to protect against neurological disease.

Probiotic

The bacteria levels in your gut play a huge role in your immune system and your body's ability to process infections and bacterias. Probiotics are really important in helping with gut health. The brain of your body.

Echinacea

This is another supplement to boost your immune system. Widely used to stave off infections and colds. Can even be used on the skin to treat wounds or infections. Available in many forms including tablets, juice, and tea.

Whilst You Eat

Whilst you eat and get dressed put on a podcast, music, audio book or some inspirational talks. Fill your mind with goodness.

Podcasts, talks and audiobooks

Here are some of my favourites.

- Impact Theory
- Sadhguru
- Eckhart Tolle
- Joe Rogan
- Success Habits
- Joel Osteen
- Elliot Hulse
- Ted Talks
- Naval
- London Real

- [Jordan Peterson](#)
- [Tai Lopez](#)
- Audible by Amazon - find some great audiobooks here

Music

If your not a big fan of talks and audiobooks then put on your favourite songs. I have a playlist for the mornings when I really need some motivation. I like to put my favourite uplifting songs here. Nothing sad or dark. Only songs that put a smile on your face and make you want to sing and dance along. Even if you can't sing or dance, do it! It will put you in a great mood for the day ahead.

Most Important Task Of The Day

Showered, dressed and ready to take on the world! By now you should not have checked any emails of social media. You are in control of your day and not in reaction.

Now is the time to tackle your most important task of the day. This is the task or activity that will create the most significant results in your life. That could be planning the day, a business task that gives the most results or even going to the gym.

Whatever is the most important thing in your life, take care of it first. Ideally it should be something that requires a significant mental focus since your brain will be in an optimal state at this point of the day.

Focus on what produces results. Not all of the activities and tasks in your life are equal. Some hold more weight than others and thus contribute to more value. You should be continuously aware of what are the most important things in your life. Personally I like to do weekly reviews of all my goals, actions and areas of my life. I can then begin to prioritize the things that matter the most. Pay attention and don't get caught up in going through the motions.

All it takes is a few minutes each day to identify the tasks which are the most important. You can then designate the time and amount of time to work on them. Then you can work your way down the priorities and any things that come up along the way. In time you will be equipped to deal with challenges and priorities.

After your morning routine create a list of the most important tasks. This could come from a master list that you set up on the weekend. Then focus on getting these done. They could be recurring activities as well. Even better if they are because it will reinforce the habit. Ask yourself, what are the most important things that I need to do today? How would they make a difference? Combine this with setting a deadline for the tasks to be done by. This will help you to complete them much quicker than you imagined. Structure your day to make sure the most important tasks are done first and then your on your way to more success.

Plan Your Day

Planning your day makes a massive difference to achieving your goals. It cuts out time wasted and allows you to focus on the activities, people and things that matter the most to you. Instead of being busy being busy and never really achieving anything plan the day before it starts and your productivity will be much higher. Ideally you should plan the night before so your mind is ready when you wake up and has more reasons to get up. But you can also do it in the morning. As you wish!

The first step to planning your day is to understand how much time you have available and when it is available. When your planning the day you need to work around the regular activities in your life such as going to work, events and so on.

Make a list of all the things you need to do. Don't stress or worry about it just let your mind release all of it. Include everything from picking up your laundry to cleaning the bathroom, working on your business, going to the gym and yeah you get it.

Prioritize your tasks and set a time for them. Decide how long they will take. Everything on any list should be assigned a time and priority. Schedule time for your, goals and projects.

Determine the outlook of your day and any open time slots for things to fit in. Most things will be recurring like going to the gym in the morning, then going to work and so on. That can come from your week plan. The day plan is where you focus in on each hour of the day. Make sure you put time in there to buffer where you get to relax or spend quality time with friends and family. Put in any activities and appointments for the day also. Its best to work in one hour time slots here.

Make use of your calendar for upcoming events and things you need to be reminded of. Be sure to check this everyday and set up reminders for the important things.

Having this plan in place doesn't mean you have to rigidly stick to it. Of course things come up during the day and we need to take care of them as they do. But by having some basic planning in place your time will be spent much more wisely leaving you fullfilled and happier.

Conclusion

Morning routines!

Now you have all you need to know to set up a good morning routine. Everything outlined in this book serves to guide you. Ultimately the best morning routine is the one that feels right for you. Choose what resonates and benefits you. What works for me might not suit you and vice versa. With your whole morning routine you want to only use the activities that benefit you the most. Maybe you can drop some that don't add value to you and extend times of others that do.

Design your own based on your needs and the kind of person you want to be. If time is tight but you need to reduce stress then just do some meditation or journaling. Or if your health conscious skip breakfast and do some Tai Chi. Over time you can review what works for you or what you might need to add. The choice is yours.

Take note of the activities you do. Take note of the times you don't do them. Track all of it, including those times when you snooze or miss something. When you start to see the wins stack up is when your habits start to form stronger. Winning early on is one step further to reaching your goals.

Start tomorrow morning and make it your morning routine a habit. You will see how much your life improves from it. The simple application of discipline to do a morning routine will give you massive confidence and self empowerment.

As each day passes you move closer to your goals and becoming the best version of yourself.

I wish you all the best!

Oscar Monfort

Thanks for Reading

What did you think of, Morning Routine: Skyrocket Your Productivity, Enhance Your Energy & Achieve Your Goals With A Fully Optimized Morning Ritual

I know you could have picked any number of books to read, but you picked this book and for that I am extremely grateful.

I hope that it added at value and quality to your everyday life. If so, it would be really nice if you could share this book with your friends and family by posting to Facebook and Twitter.

If you enjoyed this book and found some benefit in reading this, I'd like to hear from you and hope that you could take some time to post a review. Your feedback and support will help this author to greatly improve his writing craft for future projects and make this book even better.

I want you, the reader, to know that your review is very important and so, if you'd like to leave a review, all you have to do is click here and away you go. I wish you all the best in your future success!

Thank you and good luck
Oscar Monfort

Rituals Of The Rich & Famous

Success Tips, Strategies and Habits of The Rich & Famous

Get 4 new strategies every week on how to be more productive, confident, and happy.

Get Access Now

www.ingramcontent.com/pod-product-compliance
Lightning Source LLC
Chambersburg PA
CBHW021123080526
44587CB00010B/617